WHAT CHRISTIAN LEADERS AROUND THE COUNTRY ARE SAYING:

"The issues relating to global partnerships in world missions are profound and significant. Hank Paulson, a veteran of this approach, has addressed these issues head on. Must reading!"

DR. STUART BRISCOE, ELMBROOK CHURCH, BROOKFIELD, WI

"New Hope's model for international partnerships and its proven track record is the most exciting development in missions as we move into the twenty–first century."

REV. GLENN DE MASTER, EXECUTIVE PASTOR, THE CRYSTAL CATHEDRAL GARDEN GROVE, CA

"Hank has compiled a helpful and concise description of partnerships, networking, and nationals. His decades of experience provide the authority behind the text."

DR. JIM BOUCK, SENIOR PASTOR, GRACE BAPTIST CHURCH, TRACY, CA

"The case is presented with excellence while providing some very practical steps for any congregation to follow in developing their own positive partnerships."

REV. ART BEALS, SANTA BARBARA PRESBYTERY, VENTURA, CA

"For anyone working in former Soviet Union countries or anywhere in Europe, this is invaluable information to help provide appropriate ministry. It is also a wake–up call to the need for long–term relationships in many areas of our missions outreach."

MS. MARYANN SMITH, ASBURY UNITED METHODIST CHURCH, TULSA, OK

"New Hope combines three vital realities which accelerate their effectiveness. First, they know the region. Second, they work through national Christian leadership. And third, they emphasize investment in youth-the future of the new Eastern Europe."

REV. PAUL BORTHWICK, PROFESSOR OF MISSIONS, GORDON COLLEGE, SOUTH HAMILTON, MA

"With meaningful partnerships, everybody wins. The Church needs to be about the task of empowering nationals for effective ministry. Let's go, ask how we can help, and build bridges of mutual respect for the glory of God and the furthering of God's kingdom. New Hope is doing this, and doing it well."

REV. MARSHALL C. ZIEMAN, ASSOCIATE PASTOR, HIGHLAND PARK PRESBYTERIAN CHURCH, DALLAS, TX

"Partnership is the answer to effective mission and ministry in the twenty--first Century. This book is absolutely right on target!"

JIM BURNS, PRESIDENT, YOUTHBUILDERS, SAN JUAN CAPISTRANO, CA

"The old methods of missions are no longer operative today. Hank Paulson knows this well, and he has given us a workable strategic design for moving to a new level in our ministry to Eastern Europe."

C. PETER WAGNER, CHANCELLOR, WAGNER LEADERSHIP INSTITUTE, COLORADO SPRINGS, CO

"It is stimulating and offers an important contribution to the subject of partnerships."

BRUCE K. CAMP, PRESIDENT, DUAL REACH, DANA POINT, CA

"This book is a wonderful opportunity for the local church to become energized through partnering in missions. Hank has managed to bridge the gap between all of the approaches to missions with one simple concept. This book is well worth the time spent to discover this new paradigm in missions."

REV. STEVEN R. BROOKS, PRESIDENT OF THE GENERAL SYNOD, REFORMED CHURCH IN AMERICA, SENIOR PASTOR, SPRINGS COMMUNITY CHURCH, COLORADO SPRINGS, CO

"Focus on the Family has enjoyed a fruitful partnership with New Hope for a number of years now. With New Hope providing the leadership and training and we the curriculum many lives are being greatly impacted for the Lord."

SUSAN SANGUINETTI, DIRECTOR – INTERNATIONAL RELATIONS FOCUS ON THE FAMILY, COLORADO SPRINGS, CO

Global Partnerships,
Networking and Nationals

THE THIRD PARADIGM IN MISSIONS

Hank Paulson

New Hope Publishing
a division of
New Hope International
Colorado Springs, Colorado
U.S.A.

NEW HOPE INTERNATIONAL

Published by
New Hope Publishing
A division of New Hope International
P. O. Box 25490
Colorado Springs, CO 80936
U.S.A.
www.newhopeinternational.org

Design and desktop publishing: New Hope, Cluj, Romania

Printing: Alfoldi, Debrecen, Hungary
ISBN 0-9720722-0-9

CONTENTS

Foreword   ix

Acknowledgments   xi

1. Why Global Partnerships?   1
2. New Hope Partnership Model   13
3. What the Romanian Partnership Has Taught Us   25
4. Seven Principles of an Effective Partnership   45
5. Romanian Partners Speak for Themselves   51
6. Global Partnerships and the   77
   Benefits for the Local Church
7. Different Models of Partnership   83
8. How to Get Started   91

Conclusion   99

Appendix A: Discussion Group Questions   103
Appendix B: Partnership Evaluation Chart   105
Appendix C: Do's and Don'ts of Partnerships   107

FOREWORD

HOW TO USE THIS BOOK

This book is designed to be used by missions committees, foundation boards, and mission classes. I encourage you to use the summaries to help promote discussion on the issues involved. Feel free to make overhead transparencies or handouts of the summary sheets as well as the appendices.

If you did not receive a CD with this book you can order one free. It will have all chapter summaries, charts and appendices for print out or powerpoint presentation.

ACKNOWLEDGMENTS

My appreciation goes to Dr. Robertson McQuilkin, whose article, "Stop Sending Money," published in *Christianity Today*, March 1, 1999, provoked my initial letter to the editor with the seven principles mentioned in chapter 4 of this book. Dr. McQuilkin also responded to my request for input about an earlier draft, which has helped me to provide the lessons learned in a more balanced way.

I also want to express appreciation to Daniel Ricket who responded to my seven principles published in *Evangelical Missions Quarterly*, and who encouraged me to present the Romanian partnership as a present–day case study of a partnership that has lasted longer than three or four years.

Appreciation further goes to the Romanian partners themselves, whose input and opinions are expressed with sincerity and candidness.

Most of my appreciation goes to Mona, my wife and partner of more than twenty–three years, who lived with me in three countries and ministered with me in several more. Without her part, the ministry of New Hope and this book would not be what it is today.

1

WHY GLOBAL PARTNERSHIPS?

Sending U.S. missionaries to bring the Gospel to unreached people groups, as well as to countries with a significant Christian church already present, is a familiar picture to most of those in the United States. The Great Commission has been interpreted as "Americans going into all the world" with the Good News of Jesus Christ. Some churches have even gone a step further and limited their mission involvement to sending only our own people. This "send our people model" can be considered as the First Paradigm in missions.

In recent decades, international business travel and communication has grown significantly. Now many mission supporters are able to live or travel abroad and see the work personally. Through such first-hand exposure, the disparity between costs and effectiveness of an expatriate American missionary and the costs and effectiveness of a national Christian ministering, especially in third world or emerging economies, has become evident. No wonder the question is being raised: "Why don't we send our money and let nationals do the job?" This is the Second Paradigm in missions.

AMERICAN MISSIONARY EXPENSES VS NATIONAL WORKERS

AMERICAN MISSIONARY	NATIONAL WORKER
2 years Raising Support, language study and cultural learning.	0 years No support raising, language & culture training
2 years Furlough	0 years No furlough
8 years Ministry	8 years Ministry
12 years of support @ $4,500/month	**8 years of support @ $250/month**
Total = **$648,000**	Total = **$24,000**

28 National workers = the cost of 1 American missionary

Consider that the average years of service of a career missionary has dropped from twenty-two years to about twelve years. Those twelve years include two years for support raising, two years furlough, and just eight years of ministry time. Within those eight years of ministry, several years are devoted to language study, cultural learning, and adaptation.

Figuring financially, twelve years of support at $4,500 per month or $54,000 per year totals $648,000 for about eight years of ministry. For a national worker in Romania, the average is less than $250 per month. Eight years of ministry at $3,000 per year results in a total of $24,000, versus $648,000 for a Western missionary.

> *In Romania, it costs an average of $250/month to fund a national worker versus $4500/month to fund a Western missionary.*

It does not take a genius to wonder about cost efficiency. Churches find it increasingly hard to rally support for the First Paradigm of missions. It's tempting, then, to consider this Second Paradigm: "Let's just send our money and let nationals do the job."

But missions is not just about cost-efficiency. Most of all, we must consider the biblical mandate: "Go and make disciples." The scripture does not say "send dollars!" And how will it affect our churches if "Missions" simply becomes part of the budget, without any personal involvement? There is a danger that this second paradigm can encourage

> *How will it affect our churches if "missions" simply becomes part of the budget, without any personal involvement?*

the local church to grow more isolated and detached from God's work worldwide–and ultimately lose its vision, passion, and blessing for obeying God's command in Scripture.

Arguments can be made for and against both these paradigms: send our people versus send money. Advocates of the opposing positions have often caused polarization, misdirected energy and missed opportunities to further God's kingdom in an effective way. So, are there any further alternatives to be considered? Yes!

A Third Paradigm for missions is "global partnerships", active partnerships between the U.S. church and the indigenous church in a target country. This would be accomplished by working with Christian nationals to reach their own country or partnering with a national church to bring the Gospel to an unreached group of people, which could be within its own national borders or in a nearby country.

In the business community, a global perspective and global partnerships are a fact of life and increasing in significance on a daily basis. Major corporations realize that to bring quality products to market requires networking with other companies in order to be fast, flexible, and cost–efficient.

To develop computer software, companies don't have to bring people to them; they can simply connect electronically and have the product development take place where the specialist is, even if they're halfway around the world. Modern day business developments are forcing Christians to look at the big picture, to think beyond what has traditionally been done in missions, and to move beyond their own "production capabilities."

> *Global partnerships is not just a Western idea, but it is what the church in many countries around the world is asking for.*

But more important than the business model is scriptural reference regarding the importance of a global perspective and global partnerships. With fascination, I read Luke 5:4–11, the passage in which Christ called His first disciples. These men were not polished scholars of the law. They were not debating and opposing one another on theological issues. They were rough, practical fishermen working together-"networking," if you will.

When Jesus told them to throw out their nets, they heard Him and obeyed. They did not throw out individual fishing lines, like we are so often tempted to do in missions. They realized that fishing with an individual line is good for amateurs; it keeps them occupied, but it's not for professional fishermen. It will not provide a living.

Those experienced fishermen obeyed Jesus, in spite of the fact that the timing and location didn't seem to make sense to them. And see what happened? The catch was larger than they ever could have imagined–too large to bring to shore alone. What was their next move? They asked another boat to come over and help. Not only were they working together as a team in their own boat, they also were willing to partner with others and share their catch.

Global partnerships is not just a Western idea, but it is what the church in many countries around the world is asking for. This is especially true in the former Communist countries of Eastern Europe and the former Soviet Union, where suspicion is often justified regarding many foreign groups coming in uninvited.

Too often, individual churches want to be self-sufficient and work with their own individual fishing lines. Are we willing to ask another ministry, another church to come over and help haul in a bigger catch with our joint mission effort? Or are we willing to join a coalition of churches, and thereby demonstrate and model ministry partnerships?

What was it that convinced the first boat of fishermen to want to partner? I believe a major factor was that they saw how big the catch was–and how incapable they were of bringing it all home. And, being good fishermen, they preferred to share it rather than see it slip away. Often, it is the one or two fishes we see, that we are eager to claim as "our success," that prevent us from obeying Jesus' instructions to throw out our nets His way, and that prevent us from seeing how big the catch is.

With this experience in place, Jesus said, "Don't be afraid [you haven't seen anything yet]. I will make you fishers of men." This teamwork, this synergy of working together, where one-plus-one equals more-than-two is the benefit of the Third Paradigm, partnering. More can be accomplished when we back away from a view that our church or church pro-gram is the only one called to do the job.

> *First Paradigm: Send Our People*
> *Second Paradigm: Send Our Money*
> *Third Paradigm: Partnership/Send Both!*

The New Testament is a wonderful record of many different churches. The first century Christians never ignored another city's unique situation, competed for territory, or tried to be the most influential. Was each different and uniquely talented? Absolutely, but designed to complement, not compete. I read of Christ giving Himself and redeeming one church; one church that meets in many locations. I read Jesus' earnest prayer: that His disciples may be one. I read about His desire that those on the outside would mark Christians by their love among one another (John 13:34–35).

Where does that leave us? A passion for the lost and a desire to obey Christ is wonderful, but how does one person's calling fit into God's plan and into His Church? And how does our local church fit into God's Church worldwide? These are questions that make us look beyond our individual horizons to the one we all share.

> *Networking and partnering with nationals can add additional excitement and involvement to our churches.*

However, I have seen that networking and partnering with nationals can add additional excitement and involvement to our churches in the United States. At the same time, this Third Paradigm of cross–cultural partnerships brings new and different challenges. We need to be ready to handle issues like accountability, dependency, and cross–cultural differences–a potential minefield of conflicts, causing frustrations and disappointments rather than ministry success.

In the pages that follow, I share a practical case study of more than ten years of partnering in Romania. Our fellow Christians in Romania and our Western "missionaries," including myself, have learned from one another and have accomplished much more together than each of us could have on our own. We are demonstrating how to–and hopefully encouraging others to–work the net together because the harvest is beyond our individual capacity.

We at New Hope are still in the midst of the learning process. It is my desire that this reading will stimulate your thinking and that you will share with me lessons you have learned from your experience in cross–cultural partnerships. Furthermore, I invite you to join me or one of New Hope's national staff to see and experience firsthand the New Hope ministry partnerships, presently functioning in six very different countries of Eastern Europe: Czech Republic, Slovakia, Ukraine, Republic of Moldova, Hungary, and Romania.

> *We need to be ready to handle issues like account- ability, dependency and cross cultural differences*

WHY GLOBAL PARTNERSHIPS?

In a nutshell:

- ◆ Scripture encourages us to work together in unity.

- ◆ Global ministry emphasizes working together, while international expansion emphasizes one country dominating another.

- ◆ Partnerships model unity in the Body of Christ, here as well as in the field.

- ◆ Partnerships with the West is what national church leaders ask for.

- ◆ Working with nationals shows respect for their churches and culture.

- ◆ Partnerships allow each member in the Body to function in his/her area of giftedness and complement–not compete–with each other.

- ◆ Partnering with nationals is good stewardship of God's financial and human resources.

CONTINUED

◆ Nationals stay a lifetime; foreigners for just a few years.

◆ Nationals are effective from day one; foreigners have to study language and culture first.

◆ Nationals have no furloughs, and therefore no interruptions of ministry.

◆ With nationals doing the ministry, there is no suspicion of foreigners by the national church or government.

◆ National ministry models can be duplicated more easily than a ministry model operated by foreigners.

◆ Longevity and effectiveness require national ownership.

2

NEW HOPE PARTNERSHIP MODEL

BACKGROUND

When freedom finally came on December 23, 1989–after two generations of Communist domination–the Church in Romania was significantly affected. For decades, church leadership was allowed insufficient access to ministry training, while the quality of the teachers and the content were less than desirable. The Church was not permitted to have an impact beyond its own walls and was especially restricted in reaching children and youth, even its own. Church youth meetings were not permitted, while Communist party membership and acceptance of atheist doctrine provided opportunity and access to sports, higher education, and better jobs. An encouraging and sustaining factor during the totalitarian years was the clandestine ministry of countless Romanian believers who took great personal risks. Western organizations that smuggled in Bibles and literature and conducted clandestine camps and training efforts also helped.

When the doors of freedom opened, the Church was overwhelmed with all the new opportunities for ministry, but at the same time it was ill-equipped. How, for instance, could they suddenly start youth ministry without having trained workers or curriculum and resources in their own language? At the same time, New Hope International–formerly Eastern European Bible Mission–one of the organizations heavily involved in clandestine Bible and literature work, secret youth camps, and training efforts, found itself at a crossroads. When freedom came, the organization as it had functioned for almost twenty years was no longer needed. The question became: Would there be a need for New Hope International in the new political and religious climate? If so, how could New Hope best serve?

ORGANIZATIONAL PROFILE

New Hope International (NHI), located in Colorado Springs, Colorado, U.S.A., has transitioned into an exciting, new organization. It works with a small U.S. staff and a limited budget in six Central and Eastern European countries: Romania, the Republic of Moldova, Ukraine, Slovakia, Czech Republic, and Hungary, while plans are in place for ministry in other former Soviet Republics.

Goal #1: Build Bridges

NHI functions as a bridge-builder and partnership facilitator, cooperating with various U.S. ministries, as well as with cutting-edge local U.S. churches. It specializes in creating national organizations with a particular emphasis on equipping and partnering with existing national churches in the areas of children's, youth, and family ministry. Leadership development and national publishing houses undergird these efforts.

Goal #2: Mobilize National Churches for Children's, Youth, and Family Ministry

New Hope is committed to working within the existing church and denominational structures. Only in partnership with national churches does it get involved in church planting efforts–mainly through evangelistic children's and youth ministry, both in communities as well as in the public school system. Its ultimate goal is to help the church win the next generation for Christ.

> *NHI specializes in children's, youth and family ministry.*

Goal #3: Encourage National Ownership

Though New Hope gives birth to national organizations, it does so only at the invitation of national church leaders. The ministry is developed under a national board of directors and is staffed by nationals. Americans are used as non-resident missionaries with assignments to train, mentor, and encourage. Short-term mission teams from supporting churches often work alongside national staff in camps and out-reach activities. New Hope also facilitates having key national leaders visit the United States to see ministry modeled within the context of the local church. Often these internships are one week each and serve to strengthen partnerships. New Hope seeks to bring these newly formed organizations to increasing matu-rity and self-sufficiency. Throughout the ministry there is an emphasis on excellence, both in terms of staff and programs.

New Hope has a small U.S. staff, but partners with other ministries, such as Focus on the Family, YouthBuilders, BCM International, INJOY, and oth-ers to provide top resources and training for its affili-ate partners. New Hope uses an association agree-ment; a planning, financial budgeting, and reporting system; as well as other tools that are explained from the very beginning, so that both national board and staff are well aware of expectations. New Hope's emphasis is on cultivation, not domination. Its history of twenty years of service during the Communist era, with great risk and without a personal agenda, provides infallible credibility and relationships.

> *New Hope's emphasis is on cultivation–not domination.*

CASE IN POINT

Our first national partner was New Hope Romania. Its first staff person, Tavi Verlan, joined in the summer of 1990, soon after freedom came to Romania. Today, Tavi heads up the publishing portion of the ministry and is part of New Hope's staff of seven in the city of Timisoara. After a slow beginning in publishing Christian books for both the Christian and secular markets (about 40 percent is distributed in secular shops), the team's remarkable progress now includes:

1. Eighteen book titles with over 160,000 copies sold in nine years.
2. Production of sixty issues of a bi-monthly youth devotional (*Campus Journal* by Radio Bible Class).
3. Production and distribution of 360 sets of Sunday school curriculum (BCM International) now being used by over 1,000 teachers, teaching over 30,000 children weekly.
4. A project recently begun involving the translation and distribution of bi-monthly leadership tapes (INJOY by Dr. John Maxwell) with accompanying outlines–10 tapes so far.
5. Operation of a summer camp program in two different locations simultaneously throughout the summer months (seven camps total each year). Part of the objective is to provide local church volunteers with hands-on training in order to multiply

the number of camps throughout Romania. All resources for this are available on a Web site, in print, and on CD.

Besides the Timisoara team, a second New Hope team is located in Cluj, Romania. Director Rei Abrudan has nine Romanians and four Hungarians on staff locally. Besides equipping churches for youth and children's ministry among the Romanian people, the Hungarian team focuses on the two million Hungarians who form a minority in Romania. In addition, a team of three national workers in the Republic of Moldova and three Romanian staff members in western Ukraine report to Rei in Cluj.

The Cluj team is more the "research and development" branch, continually experimenting in its efforts to better equip others, especially for youth and children's ministry. Although the main effort is local church–based ministry and using that model to equip other churches, the development of resource materials, curriculum, and distribution through regional and national training conferences is an important undergirding activity in their efforts to assist and equip the Church nationwide. More than twenty youth worker books, including *The Youth Builder* series by Jim Burns and Josh McDowell's *Handbook on Youth Counseling* were translated and produced in Cluj during the last few years. A new project which began in 2000 with the translation, production, and use of *Sex, Lies and...the Truth*, a Focus on the Family product, is currently being used in

Romanian public schools as well as by church groups. Local church-based orphan ministry is another result of mobilizing Romanian churches.

The total monthly budget in 2001 for the Timisoara team is $6,160 per month, of which New Hope International subsidizes $4,250 per month—the cost of one Western missionary.

The total budget of the Cluj team (Romanian and Hungarian) is $5,250 plus $2,540, equaling $7,790 per month, of which New Hope subsidizes $7,200 per month.

The Timisoara team is very mature, stable, and dependable, but somewhat less innovative than the Cluj team. Both are very teachable and cooperative. They complement each other in a very significant way. The fact that in Cluj both Romanian and Hungarian coworkers of various denominations are benefiting from one another's experience and equipment and work cooperatively together is unique in Romania and a real testimony of Christian unity. Modeling ministry, but also modeling cooperation in an often ethnically-divided part of Europe, is essential in order for Christian values and principles to take root.

KEY PLAYERS

United States of America: Hank Paulson

I am an initiating key player in the partnerships. My role as founder and my continued involvement with New Hope since 1971, particularly during the Communist era, gave me an understanding, reputation, and relationships that were invaluable in starting and facilitating the partnership with New Hope Romania. My European background helped me to cross ethnic and denominational lines. As I come from a small country, Holland, and do not pretend to have all the answers myself, I can build bridges more quickly than if I had been an American (even though I have lived in the United States since 1993).

Timisoara: Tavi Verlan and Tinu Leontiuc

Tavi Verlan, who became the first Romanian New Hope worker in 1990 and was originally the team leader in Timisoara, is now second–in–command and responsible for the publishing department, in addition to various financial and administrative duties. Tinu Leontiuc has been on staff about ten years and has been the Timisoara team leader for the last few years. Tavi and Tinu are engineers, graduates of ATS (Advanced Theological Seminary), the graduate school of the

> *Modeling ministry, but also modeling cooperation in an often ethnically–divided part of Europe, is essential in order for Christian values and principles to take root.*

BEE (Biblical Education by Extension) program. They are also respected lay leaders in their church.

Cluj: Rei and Ramona Abrudan

In Cluj, Rei Abrudan is the key player in the partnership, though relationships are treasured and cultivated with each player on both Romanian and Hungarian teams. Rei joined the Romanian New Hope staff about ten years ago, shortly after he graduated with an engineering degree. His wife, Ramona, is an economist and a key player in the training of children's workers and, increasingly, family ministry (especially pertaining to young couples and premarital training). Besides Rei's nationwide equipping ministry, he is also an elder and was recently ordained as a pastor in his local church, where he is responsible for the youth ministry and models relational youth ministry within the Romanian church and culture. The church–based local ministry has grown from zero to 350 youth in ten years.

Without a huge international organization with numerous levels of management and central control, the global structure of NHI looks very flat–many dotted lines in the organizational structure and a sense of fluidness and flexibility. This creates an environment that encourages staff to innovate, learn, adjust, network, and function on the cutting–edge of ministry. It makes New Hope in Europe a welcomed partner, even to denominations with a 500–year history, who as a result of their great heritage often have much less flexibility and entrepreneurial spirit.

In an economy with high unemployment and average salaries of $150 per month, it has been very difficult to decrease our subsidy. On the positive side, it has been exciting to see the ministry grow nationwide and into neighboring countries in just a very short period. Ongoing partnership is not motivated by the need for financial support, but by the significant and growing opportunities for equipping churches nationwide for effective ministry to children, youth, and families.

THE NEW HOPE PARTNERSHIP MODEL

In a nutshell:

◆ Responding to a significantly felt need

◆ Functioning as a bridge–builder and partnership facilitator

◆ Using Americans as Non–Resident Missionaries (NRM) and Short–Term Mission (STM) teams to equip and work alongside national staff

◆ Explaining and agreeing upon goals and procedures from the start

◆ Modeling ministry and cooperation is essential

3

WHAT THE ROMANIAN PARTNERSHIP HAS TAUGHT US

CULTURAL AND GENERATIONAL DIFFERENCES

Cultural ways of thinking are especially different among the age forty-plus generation. They grew up under a very authoritarian system, both in public life as well as in the Church. For parents, it is very difficult to identify with all the new influences their children are exposed to. When parents grew up, there were one or two hours of Dictator Ceausescu and his wife on television and then the tube would go blank. Now Romanian kids spend more hours watching MTV than most American kids do.

Romanians, in general, tend to be extremely hospitable, which often coincides with an eagerness to please in regard to ministry expectancy. However, if they don't take ownership, they can easily be distracted and not follow through.

EVOLVING GOALS AND EXPECTATIONS

We have learned how important it is to be specific and detailed about expectations, to welcome their input, and to enter into the "give and take" of good communications and a developing partnership. As the partnership matures, less administrative micromanagement is needed. However, instead of being able to fiscally pull back at the same time, our financial involvement has grown. This is because the partnership continues to grow. First, the ministry went nationwide. Then the Romanian team took on ministry in the Republic of Moldova and in Western Ukraine. More recently, they launched and began overseeing the Hungarian ministry, at least in its beginning stages. They also developed a growing nationwide work in both Romanian–and Hungarian–speaking public schools of Romania. Our aim of increased self-sufficiency has not been met, partly due to the economic situation, but mostly due to *increased* ministry.

> *Our aim of increased self–sufficiency has not been met, partly due to the economic situation, but mostly due to increased ministry.*

Do we see the failure to reach self-sufficiency as a total defeat? Not in light of these facts:

♦ Publishing for the general market has become more self-sufficient, but strategic niche materials to equip leaders and children, youth, and family workers continue to require subsidy. It is because of the partnership that the publishing ministry can afford not only to look at sales and revenue, but at tools that have strategic ministry value (versus wide readership and revenue).

◆ Because of the partnership, local church-based ministry models now produce nationwide benefits and even have an impact beyond Romania.

◆ The long-term commitment to our partnership was essential to attract top quality nationals to lead and help the ministry grow.

SHORT-TERM VS. LONG-TERM PARTNERSHIPS

This brings us to the idea of short-term versus long-term partnerships. A short-term partnership (a better name would be a "joint project") seems a contradiction in terms, at least to those with whom we seek to partner. Whereas in the United States a partnership is often looked upon as a business effort based on joint interests, in most other cultures, partnerships are a relational commitment with a purpose beyond the relationship.

For many, *commitment* to the partnership is very similar to marriage, at least marriage from a biblical perspective. So, as in most situations, it is important that we invest time and effort in the courting/dating stage before we make that commitment. Relationships need time! I remember, as a

European, going to a Bible school in England where I was to share a room with two Americans and a Norwegian. After we dropped our luggage in the room, I heard the Americans say, "See you later, we're going to make friends in the lounge." The Norwegian and I were just introduced to a totally foreign concept: "making friends," and doing so in one or two hours, instead of over the course of years.

> *Whereas in the United States a partnership is often looked upon as a business effort based on joint interests, in most other cultures, partnerships are a relational commitment with a purpose beyond the relationship.*

Short–term partnerships? To people outside the United States, this is a contradiction in terms. It is like a short–term marriage. And who would want that?

When the word partnership is used, most non–Americans think long–term, a lifetime or beyond. There is permanency, commitment, and stability in the relationship. None of the New Hope national staff would have pursued the partnership if they had expected New Hope to walk away from it in two, three, or five years. In a short–term effort, there is little room for risk taking of any kind.

On the other hand, there definitely is value in joint projects between existing organizations for a specific task and period of time. In this type of relationship, there is little time for

growth of individuals and organizations. We should therefore look for both available competencies and a proven
track record. On the extreme end of the scale, it is like going
to a printer to get a book printed. There is little need for relational depth, and it is not expected.

Another joint project may be to do a camp or conference
together. This has a specific purpose and time frame, which
in turn can lead to a deeper relationship.

As U.S. churches or organizations develop a global partnership, the U.S. partner often wants the benefit of the joint
project, while also hoping for the spiritual enrichment that
only comes from a true and long-lasting partnership. When
we develop a joint project, the national partner may have
very different expectations or feel pushed to play the role
that is expected in order to obtain the funds or help needed.
Of course, this is more a partnership of manipulation than of
true mutual commitment, spiritual depth, and authenticity.

For us in our high-paced U.S. society and churches, it is
tempting to go for the quick fix, the exciting event, the mir-
acle pill, booklet, or video all ready and packaged for mass
distribution and instant results. It may be interesting to
note, however, that Jesus did not spend the majority of His
ministry time seeking to get maximum numbers of converts. Instead He spent the majority of His ministry on
equipping and engaging His followers. He went for quality
that in turn impacted the world, including you and me.

Relational ministry and seeking quality over quantity is more difficult to get our donors and supporting churches excited about, but it is quality that endures. And quality relationships just don't happen short-term or overnight.

OTHER OBSTACLES

Other obstacles we faced were that we did not get credible guarantees from church leaders that funds designated for one ministry would not be co-mingled with funds for other purposes. Even our best friends in leadership told me, "You just have to trust us," and, "Of course we cannot guarantee that a computer bought for translating youth materials would be used exclusively for that purpose."

So, in Romania we decided to start differently than, for instance, in Czechoslovakia. We informed leaders of various denominations of our intent, obtained their approval, and kept them informed as we proceeded. We started our own structure outside the denominations, but with a commitment to minister exclusively within and through the existing structures, while contributing to the unity among denominations and local churches, and within the churches themselves.

> *Jesus did not spend the majority of His ministry time seeking converts,*
> *but instead on equipping and engaging His followers.*

This separate structure gave the clear advantage of laying our own foundation instead of building on that of someone else who may not fully share our call, values, and burden. It also helped to put systems for accountability in place that contributed to the long-term success of the partnership.

NON-PROFIT STATUS UNKNOWN

Non-profits were new in 1990 and not a priority to the new government. It took a full year to register. At that point we learned that New Hope Romania was still not allowed to sell books, devotionals, and curriculum, so we started a for-profit company owned by the non-profit. Activities today are divided between both entities, as well as a Romanian "foundation."

> *We started our own structure outside the denominations, but with a commitment to minister exclusively within and through the existing structures.*

STAFFING ISSUES

Besides a national board, we also worked on staffing the new entity. The first recommendations came from friends with whom we had worked while smuggling in Bibles and books over many years. Often these "heroes of the faith" knew people with character (the only thing we cannot teach). These people with a commitment and proven track record in serving the Lord often did not have the needed talents themselves. They proved to be key, however, in serving as our broker (our connection) that God used.

The first person who joined the emerging ministry in Romania was Tavi Verlan, an engineer by background. During the Communist era, Christians could often study engineering, but were never promoted or paid beyond entry level salaries. Christians were not allowed in teaching or management positions. When freedom came, they were suddenly in demand as trustworthy citizens.

For Tavi, and soon after, a small team of New Hope workers, trusting NHI was a step of faith: "Will these people that say they want to help us prove trustworthy?" "Will they be around in five or ten years?" "Will they follow up on their promises and intent?" "Can I put my family and career at risk?" Unfortunately, many Western organizations moved in, but often disappeared, leaving their broken promises behind. Our broker, who had known us for many years, assured Tavi we were trustworthy.

WESTERN PARA–CHURCH SUSPICIONS

Of course, once we had established ministries in Czechoslovakia and Romania, it became much easier not only to talk about New Hope's intentions, but also to show ministry models in neighboring countries or people groups. The Hungarian Reformed bishop in Cluj was able to see what our Cluj team did in the Romanian churches and welcomed a similar partnership. Providing a relevant and needed message to the youth and those working with them was important, but equally important was our commitment to work within the existing structures.

Often we see a real suspicion towards Western para–church organizations. Leaders ask, "We have never had para–church organizations–why should we want them now?" or "Why do we need a leadership structure that potentially interferes with ours?" Often Western missions find well–established structures in the country in which they seek to minister, and often the two groups find themselves in competition instead of in partnership.

TOO MUCH ACCOUNTABILITY CAN BE A BAD THING

We were either told "Just trust us," or the opposite, "We want to be accountable and report, but you have to show us how." With the second attitude prevailing within our partnership, our Romanian partners assumed that all issues would come to me for a final decision, which of course would result in a weak organization long-term. A good example was

> *Our broker, who had known us for many years, assured Tavi we were trustworthy.*

with one of the first books on the publishing track. The team asked me which one of three suggested covers I preferred, to which I responded, "How many books do you think I will buy?" They laughed and commented, "But you are the boss." It gave me an opportunity to explain that we were all in this as partners and that neither I nor any of their team was the customer, only the people of Romania. Then I suggested, "Why don't you ask your neighbors in the apartment building you live in which book they would buy?" and they did. The challenge is to always strengthen local skills and confidence, while weakening international dependency.

Not long ago, I spent an hour and a half with our Ukraine team to convince them that it is okay to ask why. Having grown up in a very authoritarian environment, many hesitate to question a decision in any form. I went to great lengths to explain that I wanted them to do things they believe in, not because they were told to. I wanted them to learn the reason why, so they would not have to ask the next time a similar issue came up. I told them that as a leader I did not have all the answers, much less the very best answers, and needed their participation.

Although the younger staff understood, the staff over age forty often said, "We are sorry, Hank, we just cannot ask why and question you."

I responded, "Don't ask me why, say 'teach me'." Suddenly, this made sense to them. The topic emerged when I asked, "Why do you want to produce a newsletter?" Some thought I questioned them because I was upset. Of course, my intent was for them to be able to formulate their rationale and stay focused after launching the new effort.

> Often, people have to be taught that it's okay to ask "Why?"

THE CREATIVE SOUL AND COOPERATION MUST BE NURTURED

Creativity is another virtue we take for granted. Only a few years ago creativity (that is, not walking the Party line) would send someone to Siberia–one way! It's a major challenge now to encourage creativity for the benefit of the community or ministry and to foster an environment where people can develop, flourish, and reach their God–given potential.

Since they come from a very authoritarian background, it was also helpful for them to see that I had few answers, but many friends who can help. As far as family ministry was concerned, we teamed up and used many of Dr. Dobson's resources; Jim Burns and Youth Specialties for youth ministry; BCM for children's ministry; Dr. John Maxwell for leadership development; and so on.

The Communist era encouraged suspicion, division, and isolation, not an attitude of cooperation. Seeing me network and cooperate with ministries and churches has been helpful. Going to outside sources and partners allowed us to pick the very best ministry resources for meeting a particular need. It also gives the freedom to change course, if so desired.

Another thing that proved helpful was having various key New Hope leaders visit us in the United States, to see ministry modeled in local churches, to take part in the selection of resources for translation, and also to see how we operate as an organization. For some, this meant attending our U.S. board meetings and seeing how we prepare and conduct them, to see other independent U.S. ministries, and so on. It makes them (and those they represent) feel acknowledged and appreciated as equal partners and it provides their U.S. partners with firsthand, relevant input. Of course, not everyone is a candidate to visit the United States. Some may be tempted by the comforts of U.S. life or have difficulty accepting the significant economic differences.

> ...partners allowed us the very best ministry resources for meeting a particular need.

NO CASUAL WORDS

Another issue we dealt with is say what you mean and mean what you say. I have met so many Christians in

Romania that have been disappointed by half–promises that were perceived as promises by those asking for help. If we respond to a request with, "I would love to help" or "I will see what I can do," the expectation is that we will do all we can.

Along the same lines, people in Romania are very hospitable, so if you say, "I would love for you to visit," don't be surprised if someday someone knocks at your door and says, "Here we are. We finally made it." So be careful not to raise unrealistic expectations. We need to be sincere, consistent, and "easy to read"!

DON'T USE THE GOLDEN RULE

In too many cases, we are tempted to let gold rule. In other words, don't buy your way in. It is tempting to hire someone from an existing church or organization for your project and simply offer a higher salary. We have experiences both ways. One of our Ukrainian workers was offered $200 per month by another organization, instead of the $100 New Hope paid. The other mission agency, just arriving from the United States, thought $200 was a steal. We also have seen several of our staff being offered higher salaries, but their response was, "Do you think I am involved in ministry for the money?" and they firmly declined.

What made the difference? The national staff that declined the offer had a sense of ownership, a vision and calling for the ministry that outweighed the personal financial gain.

In most cultures, it is counterproductive and often even alienating for potential future partners to hire away employees. Don't let your money do the talking. It weakens the sense of partnership and joint ownership, and instead, provides a very paternal, skin–deep relationship that is ruled by personal benefits. When you are put in a position to influence salaries or benefits, make sure you get plenty of input from within the country that you work in. In the best scenario, salaries should not be a reason to either leave or join the partnership or joint project.

DIFFERENT OPINIONS REGARDING TIME, DISTANCE AND OBJECTIVES

No society seems to move at a faster pace than America. Time is money, and we don't want to waste it. It can only be spent once. Our hurried lifestyles tend to come with us as we move across into other cultures. It especially creates a tension in cultures where relationships are more important than programs. We live in a fast-paced, mobile society and, for instance, tend to think in terms of how many hours by plane-not by foot, bicycle, or even train. For us, one hundred years is a long time,

> *We need to be sincere, consistent, and "easy to read"!*

while for others, one hundred miles is a long way. It helps to keep our unique perspectives in mind.

We are accustomed to having organizational objectives; others may have relational objectives. We want to see immediate results (to report back to our sending church or organization); others seek quality over quantity and are less time–conscious. I cannot over--emphasize how important it is to seek quality, in relationships as well as ministry. Quality endures. Quality in ministry today serves as a solid foundation–a launching pad–for ministry tomorrow, or ten years from now. It boils down to our objective: Do we want to grow a squash or an oak tree?

> *I cannot over–emphasize how important it is to seek quality, in relationships as well as ministry. Quality endures.*

Another tension I have witnessed repeatedly is the American desire to see numbers as tangible and measurable results. They expect to see numbers of decisions made or better yet of converts, whereas the Europeans tend to put more emphasis on the longterm objective of making fully devoted followers of Jesus Christ. Maybe this is also more in line with Scripture, where we notice Jesus using little of His time to make converts and most of His time making disciples.

This tension in expectations can easily result in partners feeling pressured in fabricating statistics that in the end are the result of the work of God's Spirit.

As Americans, we tend to overestimate what can be achieved in ten days, while we underestimate the profound impact we can make in ten years.

WHAT HAVE WE LEARNED ABOUT GLOBAL PARTNERSHIPS?

In a nutshell:

◆ Learn how important it is to be specific and detailed and be prepared for some "give and take."

◆ Local church–based ministry models are key. They are proof within the local culture, and will be copied much more easily.

◆ Long–term commitment is essential to attract quality nationals to the ministry.

◆ In the United States, partnership is seen as a business effort based on joint interests. In other countries, a partnership is a relational commitment with a purpose beyond the relationship.

◆ Take time to "date" before making a commitment. Relationships need time.

◆ Our view of long–term versus short–term partnerships is very different from that of other cultures.

CONTINUED

◆ It is important to establish structure and guarantees for accountability and communication.

◆ Keep Christian leaders informed of your interest. Do not make them second–guess you.

◆ It helps to use a "broker" to establish the partnership.

◆ One successful partnership makes successive partnerships easier.

◆ We can discourage dependency through encouragement and empowerment.

◆ In some cultures, it must be taught that it's okay to ask why.

◆ Creativity might need to be encouraged and fostered.

◆ Networking was never encouraged under Communism and does not come naturally, especially to the older generation.

◆ Sometimes it helps to have a national intern in the United States.

© New Hope International   Colorado Springs, CO 80936

CONTINUED

◆ Say what you mean and mean what you say. Be easy to read.

◆ Be aware of cultural differences.

◆ The danger of buying your way in is a superficial relationship.

4

SEVEN PRINCIPLES OF AN EFFECTIVE PARTNERSHIP

At New Hope, we have learned that the establishment and development of a successful partnership is significantly affected by the following seven principles:

1. All members of the partnership should be fully committed to following Christ's Lordship.

2. The partnership should be based on mutual respect. In our desire to help, it is so easy to give our money, but difficult to give ourselves–to give in order to meet physical needs, and forget about emotional, social, and spiritual implications. Respect is something that needs to be earned and takes time. It is an expression of love that seeks to cultivate, not dominate. So we at New Hope have learned to keep our money until there is a mutually respectful relationship and invest ourselves first, to be humble, genuine, willing to learn, and appreciative. Respect is demonstrated in how we

treat our national partners as individuals, as well as how we treat their culture, heritage, leadership structures, and unique dynamics.

Doing things "our way" may have tempting short–term results, but without national ownership and roots, there will be no lasting value.

Doing things our way may have tempting short--term results, but without national ownership and national roots, there will be no lasting value.

3. A third element in a healthy partnership is mutual accountability that crosses the borders between us. This includes transparency, especially in financial matters. It means we don't just expect reports, but help them to organize and develop transparent reporting systems. It's amazing to see each New Hope ministry use a simple program such as Quicken in their budgeting and monthly financial reporting and how this strengthens our relationship. If we work with people of character, they will want to be transparent and will welcome our help.

4. More important than accountability between partners is building and strengthening a local accountability system. We don't want a partner to say to his pastor or elders, "I don't care what you think;

my support comes from the United States."
Instead, for the benefit of our partner and his ministry, we want to strengthen local accountability
to a church board, denomination, or, as in New
Hope's situation, a national board of directors,
comprised of recognized spiritual leaders, as well
as the local churches of which they are a contributing part. Local accountability not only helps
the target organization, it also contributes by presenting a healthy model to the culture at large. It thus
enhances their national ministry and keeps them
from being labeled as a "foreign connection" group
on the fringe of society. We want them in the center
of it all, where they can make the biggest difference.

5. Partnerships should be
long–term. Just like in
a marriage, we cannot
expect mutual com-
mitment if it's short–
term. This is especially

> *Just like in a marriage, we cannot expect mutual commitment if it's short–term.*

true in other cultures. Saying to an Eastern
European ministry leader, "We'll give you $10,000
the first year, $5,000 the second year, and you
should be self-sufficient by the third year,"
encourages him to look at our "partnership" exclusively in terms of dollars, and makes him look
over our shoulders for other "partners" from day

one. After two years, we may cut our support, but there may be four others responding to his plea. A long-term relationship with self-sufficiency as a goal should send specialists to help him develop local resources to meet his need. If we are involved in that process, it shows commitment, partnership, and a true sense of cultivating maturity, versus encouraging a beggar mentality–forcing them to go from one foreign funder to the next. For New Hope, it is exciting to see Czech churches not only meeting some of their own needs, but also financially sponsoring staff in Ukraine and sending teams from their country to help. It is another step toward self–respect and spiritual growth.

6. Partnerships should create unity and respect within the local culture. The best way to do that is to be supportive of the existing leadership structures, to meet their felt need, and to make sure they have the freedom to correct, redirect, and therefore reap the benefits of our service. We want to make sure that we don't isolate our national partner; we want to see him set up for success. Often, as a third party, I find myself in a unique position where I can either contribute toward polarization or toward unity. Of course, it should be our job to build bridges and encourage unity within the Body

> *Partnerships should create unity and respect within the local culture.*

of Christ. Doing so will also help our national partners in a most powerful way to be seen not as a threat, but instead as a help to the Church.

7. Partnerships need to have a bigger vision than their own local needs. Not only mutual commitment, but also a joint commitment to a purpose beyond ourselves, is critical in a healthy partnership. This is

> *Partnerships need to have a bigger vision than their own local needs.*

where many sister church relationships have missed their potential. Together with our Czech partners, we have developed ministry in Ukraine. Three or four years down the road, we see the Ukraine Church operating as a partner to cross geographic and cultural barriers to reach people in the smaller independent republics in the Caucuses and possibly even Central Asia. But to do so, Ukrainians need more than our money. They also need people who can cultivate, train, and assist in a joint mission endeavor. There is a lot of expertise in cross–cultural ministry and missions administration that we can contribute. This is a partnership that enriches. In the process all learn, grow, and are blessed! With our Romanian partnership, it's been exciting to see them reach out into the Republic of Moldova and Western Ukraine as well as helping the Hungarian ministry get started. Each partner contributes in his or her own area of giftedness.

WHAT ARE THE SEVEN PRINCIPLES OF AN EFFECTIVE PARTNERSHIP?

In a nutshell:

♦ Christ's lordship

♦ Mutual respect

♦ Mutual accountability

♦ Local accountability

♦ Long–term commitment to the partnership

♦ Development of unity and respect within the local culture

♦ Need for a vision and purpose beyond the partnership

5

ROMANIAN PARTNERS SPEAK FOR THEMSELVES

In the spirit of being equally valued partners, I have asked our Romanian partners to speak for themselves.

TIMISOARA

Though I asked for individual responses, the Timisoara team preferred to discuss and respond as a team to my questions. In order not to influence their answers, the team had no access to what I had written thus far.

> Q. *What do you think are the key ingredients that make the New Hope partnership work?*

A. There are several elements that make the partnership work. Here are a few of them:
- ◆ Faith in the same God and Lord Jesus Christ;
- ◆ Mutual trust;
- ◆ The same moral and ethical values;

◆ Open communication and sharing of opinions;

◆ Accountability, transparency, and fairness regarding finances;

◆ Mutual respect;

◆ Families and religious communities getting to know each other;

◆ A shared desire to work together for the spiritual benefit of the Romanian people.

Q. What have been some of the more difficult things in the relationship and how were they constructively dealt with?

A. There were difficulties due to the differences between the U.S. and Romanian laws. In time, most of them were resolved since our legislation changed. We registered as an official not-for-profit organization and moved on. Our ministry is a Romanian organization and it has to function according to the Romanian laws.

One area, not so much of difficulty but of difference, was setting the guidelines and vision of the ministry, according to the objectives of the organization. We found we needed time to clarify our mutual goals and means.

Other difficulties arose from the lack of appropriate communication. Due to distances and full schedules, communication was not always properly done. But when we got the time, good and open communication solved all the differences and prevented them from becoming problems. E-mail has helped us in the last few years to have more open and frequent communication. Clearly put, intentions, goals, and purposes represent the key elements to teamwork.

Another difference (not a difficulty) was the monthly finance report. We have to fill out one version of a report for the government and a different one for the mother organization [NHI]. But these differences were quickly resolved and we complied with the forms

> *Clearly put, intentions, goals, and purposes represent the key elements to teamwork.*

required by the U.S. organization. Everything went smoothly, especially in the last few years since we started to use a computer program for that.

Q. In what way has the partnership made a difference for your team and you personally?

A. In establishing a partnership with a mother organization, we learned a lot of what it means to operate a disciplined and accountable ministry. Accountability is a key element in our personal development as well. No one can improve by himself. We all need this element of accountability, not only before God but also before our fellow Christians.

We also grew in teamwork. The ministry is never a Lone Ranger adventure, but a common work. We learned to work together, according to personal gifts and abilities, passion and calling.

Another area of personal development is the professional one. Since we started from scratch, we needed a lot of training in the basics. This included computers, camp organization, translation, editing, publishing, marketing, distribution, subscription maintenance, and youth ministry. We learned by attending conferences and other forms of training.

> *Q. What do you observe as important issues for Americans to consider when they come to partner with Romanian churches or organizations? What do you wish they would do? Or not do? Or do differently?*

A. The first thing is to get to know the situation in Romania, and specifically, to know that the dominant religion is the Orthodox Church–which generally is very legalistic, liturgical, and externally focused. In the Orthodox faith, one enters through natural birth, not the new birth. You are a Christian because you were born in a Christian country and you will be saved, regardless of your life, if you are a member of the Church, properly baptized as an infant and buried in the Orthodox way, by an ordained priest. There are also prayers and offerings for the salvation of those who have died. The conclusion is that you do not need to change religion to get the real Christian experience.

Proselytizing is seen as dangerous and anti-Romanian.

Another thing that a foreigner must know is that there are only certain denominations recognized by the state and that a church cannot function legally outside these denominations. The goal is not control by the state, but the prevention of different cults taking root in Romania. However, there are a lot of independent churches that do not belong to any legally recognized denomination. Most function as not-for-profit organizations, which are not entitled to hold religious services, but only to have religious activities (such as youth or family counseling, camps, literature, and work with street children, the ill, and the abused). The situation of these churches is not very certain. So far, the government has not closed down any of them, but their legal status is uncertain and investing funds in their activities-building large buildings, for example-can prove risky.

Americans who want to start ministries in Romania must first establish good relations with the religious leaders. Then they should recruit Romanian staff-Christians with a very good reputation, who are spiritually mature, stable members of a church, and well-trained or at least teachable for the ministry they will be doing. They must come with a definite purpose and a very specific ministry in mind. Then they should do a thorough research of the field. Is there a real need for their ministry? Or is the need for a slightly different one? They should be flexible. Also, they should gather the information from multiple sources, not just one person.

Americans that want to start ministries in Romania must first establish good relations with the religious leaders. Then, they should recruit Romanian staff.

The people who are about to start a ministry should continually refer to their calling, skills, and previous experience to guide them. They should not start ministries because these are the latest big news or big needs in the country at that particular moment. For example, if they were not involved with children's ministry, they should not start one here just because the need in the news eases fund–raising issues. We should let those who are called to a specific ministry fill the gap.

They should not entrust funds to people without a good reputation or who seek after their own interests more than the work of God. Neither should they work with people who refuse to be accountable. Money can corrupt and we must prevent that. An honest and steady accountability system must be in place regarding finances and the results of the ministry.

Q. What are some of the best things that have happened as a result of the partnership?

A. It has enlarged our understanding about what a ministry is. We had access to equipment and staff that were not available here (at least when we started ten years ago). Before that we knew practically nothing about ministry, what a missionary organization is, how it works, what is expected from it, what is proper strategy, how to set goals and means to attain them, and how to form a vision for the next five or ten years of the ministry.

We also established, through the mother organization in the United States, good and credible contacts with American publishing houses. The mother organization makes the contacts, signs the contracts, pays the royalties, and is a warrant of the ministry that is taking place thousands of miles away. A U.S. organization that makes the connections and offers the accountability necessary for any type of ministry can move things forward more quickly and efficiently. For a foreign organization, especially a culturally diverse one like an Eastern European ministry, it is more difficult to deal with the foreign publishing houses.

This is also true about contacts with other ministries or churches in the United States. A foreign organization with no representation in the United States is practically lost and can lose a lot of opportunities for ministries simply because they do not know what is available. How can they find their way, understand and decide what are the best opportunities and resources for ministry?

Q. What appealed to you when you got started? And when was that?

A. The ministry started in 1990, shortly after the fall of the Iron Curtain. We started to work with New Hope because their type of ministry attracted us. We had these dreams before, even before we ever thought they could come true, and when the opportunity came, the match was almost perfect. Without the help, expertise, and support of the mother organization, these dreams would probably be today as they were before, just dreams.

We did not think the time would ever come that we could devote ourselves full-time to ministry, but the desire was there. We longed for more time and opportunities to work for the Lord, but there were a lot of limits. So, when the desire met with the opportunity for involvement in full-time ministry, there was little hesitation from us. The call was strong enough to recognize that it was God.

Q. What do you consider the benefits of the partnership for you and New Hope Romania?

A. We have already mentioned some of the benefits. We could fulfill our dreams and calling for the ministry because we had the much-needed help in starting. The churches in Romania could also learn much from the foreign ministers and ministries that are really committed to the work of God. They can learn from the foreigners' example of self–sacrifice and giving and the scope of their perspective, beyond their own culture, needs, and interests.

Another benefit was the fresh perspective gained from other ministries. A good example is Dr. Maxwell's training program on tapes for the leaders (INJOY). How would we have come up with these topics and this expertise by ourselves? How would we have found out about them? It does not mean that all the ideas or programs that work in the United States will also work in Romania, but when new ideas are talked over and tried, a lot of good ministry takes place and a lot of people get help.

> *We could fulfill our dreams and calling for the ministry because we had the much–needed help in starting.*

Still another benefit was the training opportunities that opened up for us. A few days at a conference or seminar, books, and resources, all help a lot. For example, Jim Burns emphasized at the youth workers training conference that the current trend in the youth and children's ministry in the United States is to involve parents as much as possible in the ministry, and how that benefits both the youth and their families. We have this same problem, and we were talking in our church about this particular need. At the conference we received very practical advice and learned from others' experience. One does not need to reinvent the wheel. A shared experience speaks volumes.

The good connection with publishers in the United States, resource developers, and outstanding authors is also beneficial for the work of New Hope in Romania. It is difficult to get to know the vast field in the United States if you live 10,000 miles away, but if you have someone there who can help select and make arrangements for copyright or other ministry-related problems, things can go smoothly.

We also learned from the personal contacts that we made with people in the United States, either on Vision Tours or on our own New Hope-sponsored trips. We get a lot of encouragement from these personal experiences, which enrich us and help us to become more spiritually mature.

Q. After more than ten years, have your expectations of the partnership changed? In what ways?

A. There really have been no changes of expectations. One good thing (from our perspective) is that from the beginning, we were consulted on every major decision about the ministry. We were not forced to start ministries that we were not prepared for or did not think were appropriate because of time, projected outcome, or money. This pattern has not changed. We openly discuss the course and goals of the ministry each

> *There is a mutual respect and trust, and everyone's opinion is respected and taken into consideration. The basis of the relationship has not altered.*

year. There have not been many changes in the relationship because we started with a healthy perspective of not doing our own thing regardless of what the mother organization wanted from us. There is a mutual respect and trust, and everyone's opinion is respected and taken into consideration. The basis of the relationship has not altered.

Q. *How has the partnership changed during these past years?*

A. The relationship became deeper as we got to know each other better and had more time for discussion and interaction. Our respect and trust grew. One very good thing is that communication is broader and more open. It is better than in the beginning, largely due to e-mail, which makes communication easier,

> *Communication is the key to a productive partnership. Only communication can cover the gaps and bridges between two cultures and ministries.*

faster, and cheaper. Communication is the key to a productive partnership. Only communication can cover the gaps and bridges between two cultures and ministries.

The ministry runs more smoothly now than a few years ago, after we gained some experience working within the budget, using the agreed–upon plans for the ministry.

Q. How has the ministry in Romania changed as a result of the partnership?

A. This is a hard question to answer since there was no New Hope before the partnership was established. New Hope Romania is the result of the partnership.

Q. What results are you seeing that you never expected?

A. We can honestly say that all the results that we have seen are due to partnership with New Hope International. More specifically:

- ◆ We have seen tremendous impact from the books we have published, especially Dr. Dobson's. The impact can be seen in the evangelical circles as well as in the general public. The books were received beyond our expectation.
- ◆ We did not anticipate how well the camping ministry would develop, how the ministry would spread to other churches and organizations. The results are beyond our dreams and each year we receive the confirmation about the good course of the ministry.
- ◆ The impact of the educational tools for children's workers, *Footsteps of Faith*, was greater and faster than we expected. The target of equipping workers with 500 sets of a four-year curriculum seemed long-term and difficult to achieve. But now the problem is that we do not have enough materials.

The usefulness of the materials and the eagerness of Sunday school teachers to get it are amazing to us. The project would have been impossible without the partnership of New Hope International.

◆ We have seen the same amazing results in response to the "Leadership Development" tapes. Since tapes are not a very popular ministry tool for sermons or lessons in Romania (people do not drive much), we thought that fewer people would use and appreciate the tapes, but that was not the case. The letters we receive and the interest that these tapes generate are very encouraging. This is another project possible only through partnership with NHI.

CLUJ

Rei, who is the leader of the Cluj team, responded to the same questions:

Q. *What do you think are the key ingredients that make the New Hope partnership work?*

A. *Finances*: If I look at all the activities that we are doing, I realize that 90 percent of them would disappear if finances stopped coming. The economic situation in Romania is not helping churches to run their children's and youth ministries (if they have them at all). I've seen it happen: When some kind of funding is coming to the church, its leadership starts to think beyond the regular services, to other aspects of church ministries and responsibilities. Of course, the best thing to do when finances are coming is to note specifically for what area of ministry the giver intends those monies to be used. Otherwise, the tendency is to put the money in the church budget and use it mostly for what the church leaders think is important.

Specialists: Even though Romanian churches have strong and committed people, we lack trained people–specialists––in specific areas of ministry, like children and youth, music, counseling, singles, women's and men's ministries. It's true that churches are trying to somehow cover those needs, but many times they are in situations in which they don't know how to start them or to keep them going. Through partnerships, we were able to bring in specialists that really made a difference in a church's ministry.

Commitment: This is a very important ingredient. It is one thing to start a partnership and another to stay in the partnership for a longer period of time. This way we can build relationships and make changes according to a better long–term understanding of the situation and of the needs that come up in the process.

Spiritual support: The first three areas that I've mentioned are not enough for a successful partnership. Spiritual support through prayer is a key ingredient. It is a special thing to know that there are people–and not just a few–that keep us and our ministry in prayer. "When we work, we work; when we pray, God works."

Cultural sensitivity: If we want to see God working in Eastern European countries, we have to be culturally sensitive. Many times people from

> *If we want to see God working, we have to be culturally sensitive.*

these countries treat the lack of cultural sensitivity as disrespect for their way of understanding or doing things.

Responding to real needs: It is almost always wrong when a church, organization, or foundation tries to push its own program over what might be better for us. The New Hope partnership was and is a success because it started as a response to the real needs, specific to each country, encouraging the nationals to develop a program, their own program. This way, there is a sense of ownership. Responding to your own needs means you are motivated to make it work.

The desire to see kids growing in Christ: The ingredients I have mentioned are not put in order of importance. That's why this last one is not the least one. It is practically the root of everything we are doing. It is the engine that pushes the "machine" to work. It is our motivation for partnership.

Q. What have been some of the difficult things in the relationship and how were they constructively dealt with?

> New Hope partnership was and is a success because it started as a response to the real needs, specific to each country, encouraging the nationals to develop a program, their own program.

A. *Financial reporting*: We as Romanians have suffered (and many still do) from a lack of order in our work. The thinking was: "This is God's money, so why should we write down all the expenses?" It seemed to be too complicated and we couldn't see the reason for it; anyway, we were not stealing God's money, after all. The partnership has helped us to keep track of all the expenses which:

◆ Showed full transparency and built trust.

◆ Made us use God's money more effectively.

Communication: During 1992–1996, we were not very good in answering back to the United States. I'm not saying now we are perfect, but we've learned to do it better. E-mail helps a lot!

Budgeting and planning ministry: Coming from a salaried background in which we were instructed, "Just do what you are told," it was pretty hard to learn how to plan for the whole year, how to make a budget, and manage cash flow. Other possible reasons for having a hard time with this issue:

◆ Fear of failing: if we plan very specifically and things don't come along as planned, failure is hard to take.

◆ No practice; when you've never done something, you need time to learn.

◆ An aversion to long-term planning, because under Communism, we were bombarded with five-year plans that were untrue and only empty propaganda.

Unprepared ministry partners: This is a thing that can embarrass both sides and puts our credibility on the line.

Learning to report in a relevant way: Americans think differently and have a different mentality than we do. So it took some time to understand and be able to report the way that is relevant for them.

Q. *In what way has the partnership made a difference for your team and you personally?*

A. There have been a number of differences for me and the team.

◆ I became more pragmatic, more goal-oriented. Americans are very practical people. Their pragmatism brings them lots of positive results in all areas of life. It influenced me to be the same way.

◆ I have been exposed to various resources and U.S. ministries. I've gotten lots of ideas from what I've seen and I have applied most of them.

◆ I've grown spiritually. Involvement in God's work is helping everyone to grow spiritually. All the preparation for talks, for presentations around the country-knowing that you are a role model for people you work with–is bringing about results. Looking back ten years, I have seen myself mature in Christ.

◆ The partnership has built confidence and motivation. We love what we are doing; we get up excited every day knowing that "this is the day that the Lord has made for us."

◆ It helped me develop a team to work with. A Lone Ranger doesn't get too far in spiritual work. We started with one person (me) and now we are thirteen New Hope workers sharing the work and the results. People on the team, as a result of partnership, succeeded in learning new things, like more quality computer work, and editing skills for the book publishing and for the youth work, skills in approaching new people and church leaders, as well as the art of communication of the Truth.

Q. *What do you observe as important issues for Americans to consider when they come to partner with Romanian churches or organizations? What do you wish they would do? Or not do? Or do differently?*

A. The first impression of most Romanians I have talked with was that Americans who came to teach us had a superior way about them that was hard to understand. Sometimes we were treated like monkeys who had just come down from the trees. They were well-meaning, I know, but they thought we were totally backward or ignorant. I think

Romanians would like to be treated like equals, especially when we realize now that in Romania there is a great spiritual depth in believers' walks with Christ, and in living out our faith.

Q. What are some of the best things that have happened as a result of the partnership?

Romanians would like to be treated like equals, especially when we realize now that in Romania there is a great spiritual depth in believers' walks with Christ, and in living out our faith.

A. *Trained nationals* in several areas of ministry: In Romania almost all the ministries, besides the Sunday services, had to start from scratch with lay people and volunteer workers. They had big hearts, but not much training. Now, after ten years, we can see a much more varied church life, and new areas of ministry—still led by volunteers, but this time trained ones, with much more confidence in what they are doing.

A vital, refreshing ministry: One truth can be said in several ways; a lesson can be taught in different ways. We've learned a lot from American creativity, and still do. The partnership brought with it a vitality and relevance in the teaching area.

Lives touched by Christ: Through the programs developed by the partnership, the kingdom of God has grown with new and young souls.

Q. What appealed to you when you got started? And when was that?

A. In January, 1992, New Hope found me doing youth ministry in my church. I was a volunteer youth worker who didn't know too much about the ministry in which I was involved. I was invited to join New Hope, but not before going through an interview. After I was asked about my vision for the youth of Romania and what would be the first steps I would take, I was told what New Hope is and what its focus is.

Three things appealed to me:

The desire to work only in and through the local existing churches: This was important to me because I was already seeing para-church organizations coming, pulling our young people out of the church life, offering them another frame in which to live their faith, as if the church is good for nothing or not able to offer them what they need. The Church needed help because there were families with young people involved, and those churches were there to stay.

Working with nationals: This kind of approach was like a revelation to me. This was the solution to equipping nationals to do the work. There are several reasons that make this approach more effective:

- ◆ No need for a visa or residence permit
- ◆ No need for years of language study

◆ No need to learn and adapt to a new culture

◆ Educating their children is no problem

◆ Never challenged by: "This may be true where you come from, but here..."

◆ Can serve for about 10 percent of the cost of a foreign missionary (considering salary, travel, ministry, and all other expenses involved)

◆ Their ministry doesn't lose them for furlough or because they don't return for a second term.

New Hope not having a program of its own: The idea of having the nationals develop a program for their own country, which they know best, seemed very healthy. Knowing the culture and the real needs of the young people, plus the feeling that the program is very Romanian, is building credibility with Romanian church leaders. I have seen some organizations that came with "the real program that works", that "has to be done" in order to see success. After they have invested lots of money in publishing their materials and in trying to introduce it in churches, it died. Nobody took the bite. Churches and people were not convinced; they'd never been asked about the relevance of the program. These three things that appealed to me were enough to say "yes" for working in this type of partnership.

Q. Have your expectations of the partnership changed? In what ways?

A. In the beginning, I didn't look too far from home. I started as a translator for the book *The Youth Builder* and did youth work in my church. My expectations were small. I was looking only in my "backyard." After the book was published, everything changed. I was contacted by other youth workers in my country, and I realized that there are others besides me who needed help, with needs that they cannot meet. In that moment, I understood that the partnership could bring a breath of fresh air in Romania, that we could meet those needs. In that moment, my expectations changed. I've seen that through the partnership, we can bring specialists to train other youth workers and that we have to find supporters to help with publishing resources. Later my expectations looked forward: Why not expand into other countries where people also speak our language? Sometime during this process, the partnership offered me the opportunity for travel in the United States. The visit showed me new ways to improve myself and my ministry, and, as a result, to bring new things to my country.

> Q. How has the ministry in Romania changed as a result of the partnership? What results are you seeing that you never expected?

A. I guess, as a result of the partnership, the ministry in Romania has grown in a number of churches. More and more churches are realizing how important children's and youth ministries are, and they are opening their doors to it. Anyway, I dream big and my expectations are not all fulfilled yet. It's getting better, but there is much more work to be done.

Q. What would be your advice to someone who wanted to start a cross-cultural partnership?

A. I would very much suggest considering the seven key ingredients mentioned earlier. I would also like for them to realize that a partnership supposes something that goes in both directions: giving and getting. If their main thinking is what can I get from it?, then very soon the relationship will be broken. I would like to remind them that the lowest level of Christianity is to be blessed; the highest level is to be a blessing!

> *A partnership supposes something that goes in both directions: giving and getting.*

WHAT ARE THE ROMANIAN PARTNERS SAYING?

In a nutshell:

◆ Understand the local legal, cultural, and church situation, or ask about it.

◆ Accountability is a key element in personal development as well as for the partnership.

◆ Recruit and encourage nationals in their area of giftedness, not just in the areas of organizational need.

◆ Work with people whose reputation is above reproach. Check them out first.

◆ Partnership enlarges the horizon for both partners.

◆ A mutual respect and trust is needed from the beginning.

◆ Specialists are needed who can treat the national partners as equals.

CONTINUED

◆ Respond to real felt needs, instead of pushing your program.

◆ Work with nationals to help them develop their own programs.

◆ Encourage national ownership.

◆ Exposure to U.S. ministry models is much appreciated.

◆ A desire to work only in and through the existing local churches will open doors and has the greatest long–term strategic potential.

6

GLOBAL PARTNERSHIPS AND THE BENEFITS FOR THE LOCAL CHURCH

KEEPING THE CUTTING EDGE

In the First Paradigm–sending our own missionaries for career ministry overseas–supporters often stay connected long-distance, by occasional visits, and by hearing the reports of language study, cultural adjustments, mistakes, and difficulties as well as ministry results. In some cases, short-term mission teams can come and minister alongside their long-term missionaries.

In the Second Paradigm–sending money only and letting the nationals do the work–there is little connection, though potentially great ministry in the field.

The Third Paradigm–partnering with nationals for ministry in their own country and culture or for the purpose of teaming up to minister to an unreached group of people together–not only benefits the joint partnership objectives and the overseas ministry partner, but also the church in the United States. If done correctly, the partnership provides an exciting ministry model as a complement, not an alternative, to sending Pauline–type cross–cultural missionaries. The partnership model appeals to the younger generation, as well as to the business community, which is growing more global every day. It gives them a sense that missions in the church is innovative, willing to experiment, and will stay on the cutting edge where they can do the most good.

The partnership model appeals to the younger generation, as well as to the business community, which is growing more global every day. It gives them a sense that missions in the church is innovative, willing to experiment, and will stay on the cutting edge where they can do the most good.

WISE STEWARDSHIP IS REWARDING

Computer giants like IBM and Hewlett Packard don't even consider producing their own product at headquarters. The machine I work on is the result of a global partnership that combines screen, hard disk drive, CPU, and a long list of software components from various suppliers from across the globe. When I buy a car, the documentation tells me where it was assembled and the percentage of parts made in the United States. In missions, we are often slower to adjust and think globally. For many, the Great Commission is not just about "going and making disciples of all nations," but about supporting our people overseas, while we are afraid of asking questions about efficiencies and potential alternative models of "making disciples of all nations."

The New Hope partnership model benefits the local church, because it sends a message to the congregation that the church takes financial stewardship seriously in all areas of ministry, and members will be delighted to see their giving go very far in terms of results.

HANDS-ON INVOLVEMENT IS WELCOMED

Connection is essential for a partnership to come alive and be a long-term success. The New Hope partnership provides connection opportunities on many levels, involving all kinds of different people as short-term missionaries (STM) or non-resident missionaries (NRM). Members of the staff and Sunday school teachers can be involved as trainers. High school and college groups can work alongside nationals in conferences, camps, and outreach. Professionals can be involved to train and mentor in leadership, computer skills, medical needs, music and the arts, and other areas of felt need.

> *Connection is essential for a partnership to come alive and be a long-term success.*

Another relationship builder is to have your national visit your church in the United States to see ministry modeled, and to share with individuals and groups within your church. (Be careful, though, that your national partner is able to handle the U.S. standard of living and comfort and is willing to return to his home country, positively affected by his or her U.S. experience.) The U.S. visits can provide connection, excitement, and ownership to those not able to travel overseas, while it can help prepare and build the bridge for others to travel and minister alongside the national, helping to implement the relevant things seen modeled.

A SPIRITUAL BLESSING TO ALL

Most of all, it benefits everyone spiritually to see the Body of Christ come together and members from different cultures work together, complementing each of them in their area of giftedness, under Christ's all–encompassing lordship. As different parts of Christ's Body, we can and should recognize each other, respect each other, and cooperate in sharing the Good News. This is a testimony and encouragement not only to the church members, but also to those outside the church, here as well as overseas.

> As different parts of Christ's Body, we can and should recognize each other, respect each other, and cooperate in sharing the Good News.

It also helps us in the United States to learn from the testimony of others who have suffered for their faith. It helps seeing our situation from a different perspective and being assured of God's provision and presence even in the severest of difficulties.

WHAT ARE THE BENEFITS FOR THE LOCAL CHURCH?

In a nutshell:

◆ Missions efforts feel innovative, fresh, and vital when they stay on the cutting edge.

◆ Stewardship is taken seriously.

◆ Connection between the mission work and the local U.S. church makes the partnership come alive and improves the chances of long–term success.

◆ A spiritual model of the Body of Christ working together.

7

DIFFERENT MODELS OF PARTNERSHIP

DEFINING PARTNERSHIP

The word "partnership" can be confusing or enlightening. Tokumboh Adeyemo, a prominent African church leader and theologian, identifies seven distinct forms of partnership [taken from William Taylor's book, *Kingdom Partnerships for Synergy in Missions*]:

Mother–daughter partnerships: A mission organization initiates and then maintains ongoing domination of the relationship. Issues of control and independence continually pervade this relationship.

Entrepreneurial partnerships: A mission organization employs "nationals" to carry out its objectives. Dependency, domination, and ownership by the funders characterize this relationship.

National support partnerships: A mission organization funds a national ministry. Money tends to define the relationship and both groups may feel used by the other.

National team partnerships: Multi–national teams are formed with each having equal authority and responsibility. Unfortunately, over time, the team tends to develop the personality and leadership style of its most affluent member.

Paternal network partnerships: Non–Western organizations receive financial support from Western mission organizations. Though the non–Western ministry controls financial decisions and program development, the systems of reporting and accountability required by the donors may feel paternalistic.

Short–term partnerships: A Western mission organization may provide temporary staff and funding requested by a non–Western ministry. Though this avoids long–term domination and dependency, its brevity inhibits genuine mutuality and relationships.

Multi–national church network partnerships: Participants perceive themselves as equal members of the Body of Christ. Each brings strengths and needs, resources and vision to the partnership for the mutual enrichment of the Church.

New Hope's partnership started as an entrepreneurial partnership, though with the important difference that we did not impose our objectives but responded to felt needs and mutually agreed-upon objectives. This allowed the partnership to transition into a more mature "mutually transforming global partnership." Though the mutually transforming global partnership is similar to the multi-national church network partnership, in which members consider themselves equal and mutually beneficial, resulting in transformed lives on both sides of the partnership, the New Hope model is different as it has a purpose beyond the partners themselves—an outward-looking global perspective.

Initially, the New Hope partnership was between the Romanian partner and the U.S. New Hope organization. Increasingly, NHI has become a broker, facilitator, bridge-builder, and mentor for cutting-edge U.S. churches to take over New Hope's end of the partnership. This is the model that New Hope considers the ideal.

> *Increasingly, NHI has become a broker, facilitator, bridge-builder and mentor for cutting-edge U.S. churches to take over New Hope's end of the partnership. This is the model that New Hope considers the ideal.*

Though a long-term relationship is desired, it can also sound intimidating or otherwise not desirable. For this reason,

New Hope also facilitates sponsorships of one– time needs or adopting a national staff worker in, for instance, Ukraine, for just $80 per month salary and $80 per month ministry expenses.

GLOBAL PARTNERSHIPS TO REACH THE UNREACHED

The Perspectives courses, a series for orientation and training on missions taught throughout the United States, have been of incredible importance to the U.S. church in recent years. They have brought a depth, commitment, and understanding to a broader audience than ever before. I have been privileged to teach some of the classes myself. Still, in the presentation of evangelism and growth, the courses come short on the concept of Global Partnerships as outlined before.

Very effectively, it presents church growth in four steps:
1. Internal growth.
2. Expansion growth of the local church.
3. Extension growth, mostly by producing daughter churches.
4. Bridging growth, by extending its witness and church–planting efforts, bridging barriers, and establishing growth in areas where the culture has more in common and where there are fewer barriers to cross. And bridging even more barriers as it extends into unreached people groups.

I would like very much to encourage a fifth step by means of the Global Partnerships model, where the U.S. church and the church in a different culture team up, complement each other, and make a joint impact in the target area.

In recent years, we have seen U.S. military success, especially where it built coalitions, alliances, and partnerships. It has strengthened the impact, aided both from an intelligence, as well as from a logistical point of view.

In the same way, when we partner globally, it multiplies the impact of our mission efforts. It helps us to be more culturally sensitive, as part of a multi–cultural effort. It also helps us complement each other's gifts and it demonstrates to the unreached people group that Christianity is not just for Lone Rangers, each establishing their own ethnic denomination, but for communities of diverse people groups.

This joining up to reach an unreached people group is an area New Hope has hardly touched on itself. Some very rewarding mission efforts are taking place from the Czech Republic, Slovakia, Hungary, and Romania into Ukraine and the Republic of Moldova. I look forward to the day that

> *In recent years, we have seen U.S. military success, especially where it built coalitions, alliances, and partnerships. It has strengthened the impact, aided both from an intelligence, as well as from a logistical point of view.*

we can train, partner, and help the church in Ukraine to send out its missionaries to unreached people groups in the Caucasus and other parts of the former Soviet Union, or maybe even beyond.

It may be easier for us to organize a coalition of American organizations. Though this is a positive demonstration of unity, and often a better use of resources by its sheer size and amount of available dollars, it easily loses cross-cultural sensitivity. I have often been told by national Christian leaders in Eastern Europe and the former USSR that when freedom came, they felt steam-rolled by the large number of outsiders coming to their country and that their opinion was often of little consideration. If we take a learning, serving, and empowering posture, the long-term impact can be so much greater.

> *If we take a learning, serving, and empowering posture, the long-term impact can be so much greater.*

DIFFERENT MODELS OF PARTNERSHIP

In a nutshell:

◆ Different forms of partnership have their potential strengths and weaknesses.

◆ Partnerships can and should be mutually transforming.

◆ Partnerships are possible to meet a need in the partners' culture or can have a purpose beyond.

◆ A U.S. coalition of churches or ministries presents both strengths and potential pitfalls (see Appendix C).

8

HOW TO GET STARTED

PHASE ONE: BEFORE YOU GO

1. Study the topic of partnership.

> With a committee, small group, or Sunday school class, study the partnership idea, the issues involved, the advantages and disadvantages, what model would be best to pursue, what part of the world, who could help you, and how it would effect the church members, the staff, and their possible time. Make sure that during this initial phase, you involve your senior pastor and the church leadership.

2. Develop a focused prayer initiative.

> Keep this as your foundation throughout the process and partnership.

3. Identify a potential area, partner, and broker.

> Select a potential target area, potential partner(s), and a broker to help your partnership be successful right

from the beginning. Check out a potential partner or broker's credentials and track record, and ask for referrals, especially regarding your partnership broker. He or she can expedite the process, build the right connections, and also help you as you move along.

Make sure your broker or partnership facilitator is committed to your success, and is visionary, creative, and spiritual. Probably his or her most important quality should be an ability to listen, learn, and observe. He or she should demonstrate a desire, motivated by Christ's love, to cultivate, not dominate.

4. Consider your objectives for the partnership.

Does your denomination or church want to develop daughter churches? Or are you willing to help existing churches to plant their affiliates? Are you concerned about denominational color or are you willing to help various denominations, including indigenous ones? Which issues and values are absolute and which are negotiable? Are you limited to church planting? Or are you willing to help in areas of church growth, leadership development, children's, youth, or family ministry? Do you prefer to have "your own" partner? Or are you open to the idea of joining with one or more churches from your area in a joint partnership: a coalition of churches or a coalition of local church-based youth ministries?

5. Consider what you can bring to the partnership.

Consider your potential contribution to the partnership in terms of staff time, short-term teams, a national being an intern for one or more weeks, and your financial commitment. Though caution should be considered regarding financial help in the beginning of the partnership, it is important to establish a framework of what the partnership may cost, both in terms of people as well as financial resources. Adopting a New Hope team in a region in Romania or Ukraine could cost about $5,000 per year initially, and could easily grow to $10,000 or more after two or three years (not including your staff time and travel expenses).

PHASE TWO: MAKE YOUR FIRST MOVES

1. Check out the lay of the land.

A Vision Tour or Joshua and Caleb experience could be the next step. Here you can test your desires and assumptions by studying existing partnerships and interacting with potential future partners. New Hope organizes four Vision Tours each year where both national staff and national church leaders are visited. In addition to the Vision Tours, there are also Joshua and Caleb trips specifically for youth pastors, family workers, or others with a specific ministry interest. These Joshua and Caleb trips include hands-on ministry and interaction.

2. Report to and educate the church.

There is no better time to start getting the church at large aware and involved than after you can report first-hand. New Hope or a visiting national can assist in this process, but the leadership in this is with the church.

3. Develop and agree on joint objectives, strategy, values, and timeline.

It is now time to go to the next step by putting together joint objectives, strategy, values, and timelines. Mutual agreement of the partners and the broker are essential. You may want to consider issues such as the following: What will happen if the leadership or condition of the church, coalition, or partnership changes? Is there a time that allows you to walk away? To what extent can the broker facilitate a transition?

It's important to have an agreement or covenant in writing during the first phase of the partnership, or, better yet, at the front end. New Hope, if chosen as a broker, can help with the initial covenant, training, periodic reviews, and reporting tools. There is no reason to reinvent the wheel.

> *If your goal is lasting impact, remember that it is better to do one or two things right than to be all over the place.*

PHASE THREE: BRING THE PARTNERSHIP TO MATURITY

1. Increase hands-on involvement.

The exciting phase of personal ministry involvement starts here. Now it is time to have a national, or if that is not possible, your broker, visit or revisit your church and get your people educated, mobilized, and involved to meet specific areas of need. Encourage more than financial investment. Relationships in other cultures also need communication, joint ministry, and the expectation that, in time, both the ministry and partnership relationship will grow.

Besides people with ministry skills, there is also a felt need for U.S. partners to come alongside as mentors and executive coaches, to help develop national leaders in areas like planning, budgeting, people development, conflict resolution, and a score of other practical leadership skills. Probably one of the biggest challenges in the partnership is to stay focused. If your goal is lasting impact, remember that it is better to do one or two things right than to be all over the place.

And all along, keep evaluating, communicating, and encouraging one another. Celebrate successes!

2. Educate and increase church awareness.

This process will never stop. At a certain point, you may consider presenting special projects to various groups within the church, which will serve both to educate and connect them, as well as to get the funding for those projects. As an example, you may want to present a "national sponsorship" to a Sunday school class, have the children raise funds to send orphan children in Romania or Ukraine to a Christian camp, or purchase tents or other equipment for the camp. And all along, work on two-way communication.

With increased ownership and involvement of the church, probably the two most challenging areas will be staying focused and communicating. Again, New Hope or your partnership broker should continually be involved. It requires our most precious commodity-time!

HOW DO WE GET STARTED?

In a nutshell:

- ◆ Count the cost before starting and look at the benefits.

- ◆ Develop a potential plan.

- ◆ The key to your success is a broker with proven credentials.

- ◆ Visit your potential missionary partner.

- ◆ Invest more time than money.

- ◆ Agree on the game plan and rules before you commit.

- ◆ Make sure you have a clear purpose–a genuine calling–beyond the relationship.

- ◆ Get the church leadership on board or don't proceed.

CONTINUED

◆ Focus and rally around those things each does best.

◆ A key to long-term success is getting your people involved.

◆ Stay focused on vision and goals and communicate constantly.

CONCLUSION

It is my hope and prayer that you don't feel overwhelmed, but rather stimulated and encouraged in pursuing your first steps on the road of a Mutually Transforming Global Partnership.

After more than ten years, I offer New Hope's Romanian Partnership model not as the "perfect model," but one that can be learned from. Among six countries in which New Hope works, I chose the Romanian one because it is the oldest model, but you are invited to study each of the six in more depth.

Much is written about partnerships, but practical models are not often shared. Usually the entrepreneurs and visionaries are willing, but simply too busy to share. I hope, however, that those who read this are encouraged to share their experiences, so we can all continue to learn. I need and value input and feedback, both from U.S. churches and ministries, as well as from global partners and those involved in ministry.

> *It takes time, skill, and effort, but partnerships are the most powerful servants to the Church in the twenty–first century.*

In no way do we pretend to have all the answers. We continue to listen, learn, and improve. I also appreciate our Romanian partners for sharing and being vulnerable and transparent.

It takes time, skill, and effort, but partnerships are the most powerful servants to the Church in the twenty–first century.

For more information, dates of Vision Tours, or other opportunities, you can visit New Hope at www.newhopeinternational.org.

I value your response to the following questions. Please e-mail me at: info@newhopeinternational.org.

ONE MINUTE QUESTIONNAIRE:

1. The most helpful section in this book was:

2. In your next edition, add more on:

3. We are:
      ___ exploring partnerships
      ___ somewhat involved
      ___ heavily involved

4. Geographic area of interest or involvement:

      ___ Europe (including Eastern Europe and the former Soviet Union)
      ___ Latin America
      ___ Asia
      ___ Africa

Name: _____

Church/Organization: _____

Address: _____

City, State, Zip: _____

E-mail: _____

Web site: _____

APPENDIX A

DISCUSSION GROUP QUESTIONS ABOUT U.S. INVOLVEMENT

1. In the New Hope partnership model, is there still a need for American missionary involvement or is money the only thing the national partner needs?

2. What type of personal involvement from the United States is still needed? And is it welcome?

3. With non–resident missionaries (NRMs) who are members of a U.S. church or ministry making short–term trips overseas as part of a long–term partnership, what are the advantages or disadvantages for the national ministry? What is the impact on the quality of our contribution? On the NRM's family and support system? Would it be easier to send top specialists with proven track records as NRM's to equip nationals and function as executive coaches, or send resident with equal expertise? What are the advantages and disadvantages?

4. Does it make a difference whether we send NRM's to developed areas of the world with established national churches or send them to underdeveloped areas where there is no Christian witness? If so, how?

5. What are some of the advantages and disadvantages of having national partners intern for short periods of time in our U.S. churches?

6. How can we best prepare nationals for coming here? What can they learn while here? What can we learn from them?

7. In what ways can national partners and NRM's increase missions excitement and involvement within U.S. churches so that churches will not feel left out and end up with an "only my money is needed" syndrome?

8. What are some of the critical issues New Hope's Romanian staff warns against or appreciates?

9. In the model of New Hope Romania, what are the unique strengths and benefits of Romanian nationals and of U.S. non-resident missionaries?

10. What steps can a local church take to avoid some of the dangers and disappointments? Can we be involved in a national partnership with a small commitment focused on an individual or specific need? Where do we start?

© New Hope International   Colorado Springs, CO 80936

APPENDIX B

PARTNERSHIP EVALUATION CHART	UNACCEPTABLE	NEEDS WORK	SATISFACTORY	GOOD	OUTSTANDING
Fully devoted followers of Christ					
Theologically compatible					
Reputation of integrity					
Mutual respect between partners					
Mutual respect for culture and tradition					
Mutual blessing					
Mutual accountability					
Long–term commitment					
Contributes to the unity and respect within the local Christian and secular community					
A vision and purpose beyond the partners					
Clearly defined objectives					
An acceptable evaluation process based on objectives, not person-alities					
Commitment to communication					
Owned and endorsed by the church leadership					

Follow–up needed regarding:

Person responsible:

Time frame for action and follow–up evaluation:

Date and person(s) conducting this evaluation:

APPENDIX C

DO'S AND DON'T'S OF PARTNERSHIP

DO's	DON'Ts
◆ Listen and learn	◆ Pretend to know it all
◆ Be a servant	◆ Tell them what to do
◆ Develop self–worth/pride	◆ Act as if our culture is superior
Develop self–reliance	◆ Keep them dependent
Make a long–term commitment	◆ Go short–term while expecting loyalty
Contribute to unity within the local culture and church situation	◆ Have them go against their culture and church leadership
Make them fishers of men	◆ Make them fishers of dollars
Model how partnerships work	◆ Tell them they don't need others outside of you and them
Develop national ministry models	◆ Just tell them to copy how things are done in the United States
Share objectives and expectations from the beginning	◆ Just see what happens

DO's	DON'Ts
◆ Establish rules for accountability and transparency	◆ Wait and see
◆ Establish a process of evaluation and communication	◆ Wait and see
◆ Creativity, problem–solving, and self–reliance should be encouraged	◆ Provide all the answers and resources needed
◆ Show respect for culture and tradition	◆ Tell them how you do things in the United States
◆ Take time to explore a relationship	◆ Jump into it to save time
◆ Keep Christian leadership in the host country informed	◆ Give them reason to second–guess and mistrust your intentions and programs
◆ Maintain a balance between being sensitive to both relational as well as purpose driven issues	◆ Go all out for working with only the people with whom you feel good about or share objectives
◆ Partner with other U.S. churches *to model cooperation*	◆ Partner with other U.S. churches *to gain a strong negotiating position*

© New Hope International   Colorado Springs, CO 80936

ONE MORE WAY TO HELP YOU GET STARTED

Request additional copies of **Global Partnerships**
...for single copies, a suggested donation of $14.95 each;
...for 3 or more copies, a suggested donation of $8.95 each;
...for 10 or more copies, a suggested donation of $7.50 each.
Your donation includes the cost of shipping in the United States
and Canada.

Copy and complete the form on the next page and mail or fax it to:

> New Hope International
> PO Box 25490
> Colorado Springs, CO 80936
> USA
>
> (800) 297–9591 phone
> (719) 577–4453 FAX

You can also order through our Web site or e–mail us:

> www.newhopeinternational.org/bookorder
> info@newhopeinternational.org

PERSONAL INFORMATION

NAME: _____

ADDRESS: _____

CITY: _____ STATE: _____ ZIP: _____

E-MAIL: _____ PHONE: _____

SHIPPING ADDRESS (if different from above address)

NAME: _____

ADDRESS: _____

CITY: _____ STATE: _____ ZIP: _____

QTY	DESCRIPTION	SUGGESTED DONATION	TOTAL AMOUNT
	Global Partnerships 1 OR 2 BOOKS	$ 14.95 each	$
	- 3 OR MORE COPIES	$ 8.95 each	
	- 10 OR MORE COPIES	$ 7.50 each	
	Free CD with Overheads & Handouts	FREE	$0.00

ADDITIONAL GIFT IN SUPPORT OF N.H.I. $

TOTAL DONATION: $ _____

METHOD OF CONTRIBUTION

☐ My check payable to New Hope International is enclosed

☐ Please charge my ☐ Visa ☐ MasterCard ☐ American Express

☐☐☐☐☐☐ ☐☐☐☐☐☐ ☐☐☐☐☐☐ ☐☐☐☐☐   ｍ ｍ ｙ ｙ

CREDIT CARD NUMBER   EXPIRATION DATE

Signature _____

☐ I recommend you send a complimentary copy of your book to:

NAME: _____

ADDRESS: _____

CITY, STATE, ZIP: _____

I think this person would appreciate the book because:

_____

ECFA MEMBER — EVANGELICAL COUNCIL FINANCIAL ACCOUNTABILITY